NATIONAL GEOGRAPHIC

T0308161

Symbols of FREEDOM

PATHFINDER EDITION

By Frank Mills and Meg Runyan

CONTENTS

The Face o

f Freedom

An enduring symbol of freedom and democracy, the Statue of Liberty has welcomed immigrants to the United States for over one hundred years. Take a tour of Lady Liberty, and find out why her power endures.

By Frank Mills
Deputy Superintendent
Statue of Liberty National Monument

Perfect Spot. *Artist Frédéric-Auguste Bartholdi picked this island in New York Harbor for his famous statue.*

I live and work at one of the coolest places on Earth—the Statue of Liberty. I take deep pride in looking after this great, green lady. I help make sure she's at her best for the thousands of people who come to see her each and every day.

That's important. After all, Lady Liberty is more than a tourist **attraction**; she's a vital symbol of the United States.

The statue stands for Americans' right to be free. Dedicated on October 28, 1886, she was a gift of friendship from the people of France. The idea for the statue came from a man who believed that the United States was a shining example of **democracy** at work. Today, the Statue of Liberty remains a symbol of that idea.

Join me on Liberty Island for a closer look at this beloved American symbol.

Meet Lady Liberty

To reach Liberty Island, you need to take a ferry from New York or New Jersey. Then I'll join you, and we'll walk around the island until we face the statue.

You will need to tilt your head back to see her, because Lady Liberty is huge. At 46 meters (151 feet) tall, she is the largest metal statue in the world.

Let's start by looking at Liberty's left hand, which holds a tablet. On the tablet is the date of our nation's birthday: July 4, 1776.

Now switch to looking at Lady Liberty's right arm and follow it high into the sky. You'll see a torch with a golden flame. The torch **represents** the light of freedom. In fact, the statue's original name was "Liberty **Enlightening** the World."

Now take a look at the crown on Liberty's head. There are seven sun-like rays extending from it. They stand for liberty shining on Earth's seven continents.

It's hard to see from the ground, but there are broken chains beneath Lady Liberty's sandals. They symbolize breaking free of **tyranny**. Tyranny is when a ruler has all the power and the people have none.

Now let's go into the museum at the bottom of her pedestal, or base.

The Statue's Story

In the museum, you will see a full-size copy of Lady Liberty's foot. She wears a size 879 shoe! Like the rest of the statue, Lady Liberty's foot is made of copper.

Making the statue took more than 300 sheets of copper, which workers in France hammered by hand. The French people were so excited about the statue that they actually paid to watch the workers. When the painstaking work was done, the metal was as thick as two pennies.

After completing the statue, workers packed her into 214 crates and loaded them on a ship bound for the United States. People across America, including children, gave money to build the pedestal that the statue stands on. One girl even emptied her piggy bank and donated all the money.

Putting the statue together was like a giant jigsaw puzzle, and solving that puzzle took months. Because some pieces were labeled wrong, workers sometimes tried 20 different pieces before finding the right one.

Building Liberty. *This painting shows Lady Liberty being constructed in Paris, France.*

Old Metal, New Meanings

Now let's climb to the balcony, which runs all the way around the pedestal. From here, you can see lots of ships in New York Harbor.

Back when Lady Liberty was built, ships in the harbor carried millions of immigrants coming to live in America. My mother was one of them. Lady Liberty was one of the first things she saw. To Mom and many others, the statue came to symbolize hope for a new life and a new land.

More recently, after the attacks of September 11, 2001, I watched Lady Liberty take on yet another role. This symbol of freedom and democracy gave visitors comfort and reassurance. "America stands," she seemed to say. "We are still free, still strong."

When visitors saw the statue, their tears gave way to smiles. I can't tell you how often I saw that happen. That's the power of Lady Liberty!

Well now, you've seen the statue and you've heard her story. I hope you can see why she means so much to me—and to America.

Wordwise

attraction: something interesting that people want to see or do

democracy: a form of government in which people choose their leaders by vote

enlighten: to give knowledge or insight

represent: to be a sign or symbol of something

tyranny: a form of government in which one person rules

★ ★ ★ ★ ★ ★ ★ ★ ★

JOURNEY TO America's Capital

About 230 miles south of the Statue of Liberty lies Washington, D.C., the nation's capital. Like Lady Liberty, the capital and its monuments serve as an inspiration for millions. Roughly 16 million people visit each year!

Most head toward places shown on this map. Many famous sights lie between the Lincoln Memorial (far left) and the U.S. Capitol (far right). If you visited the city, what places would you want to see? Why?

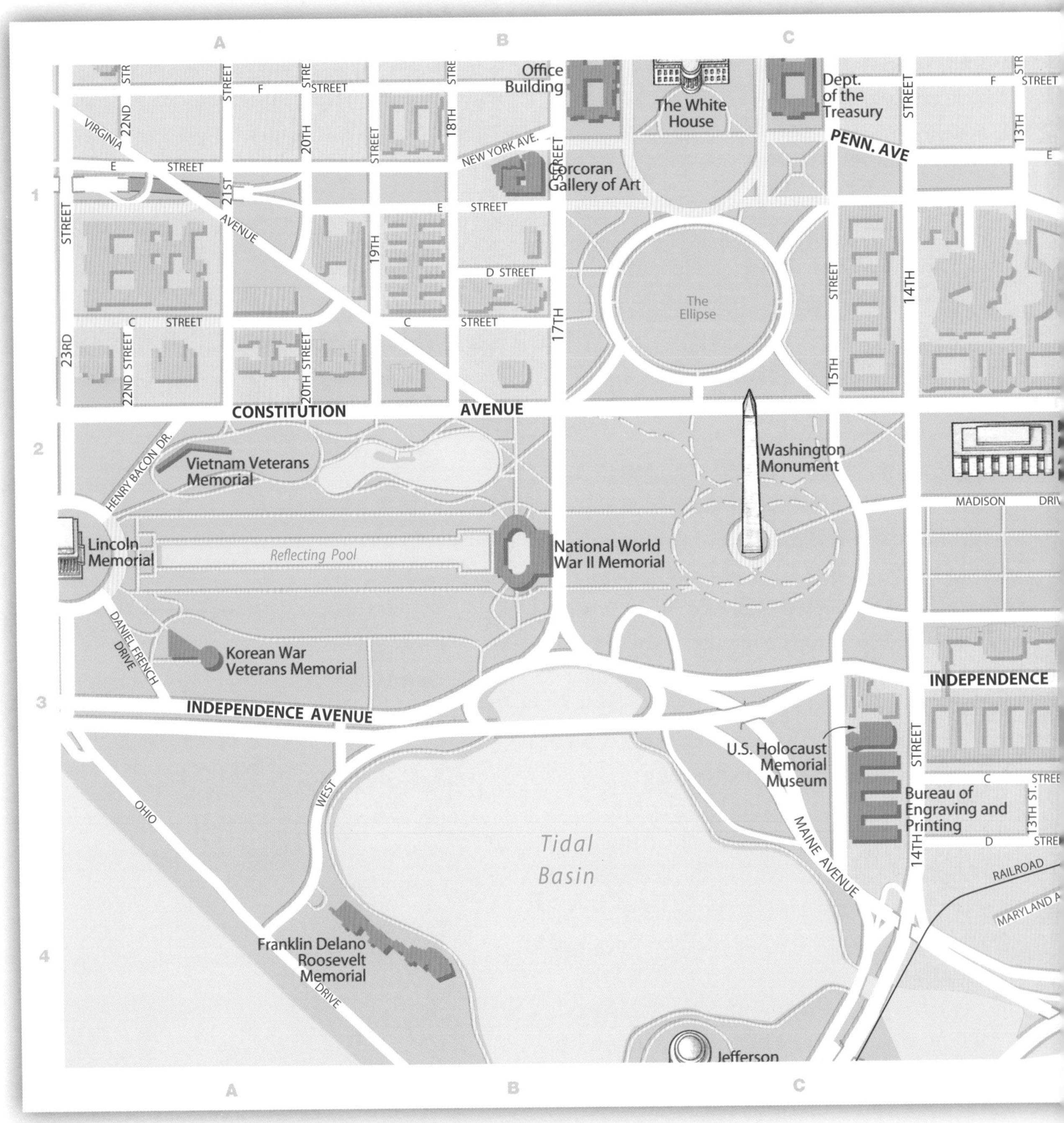

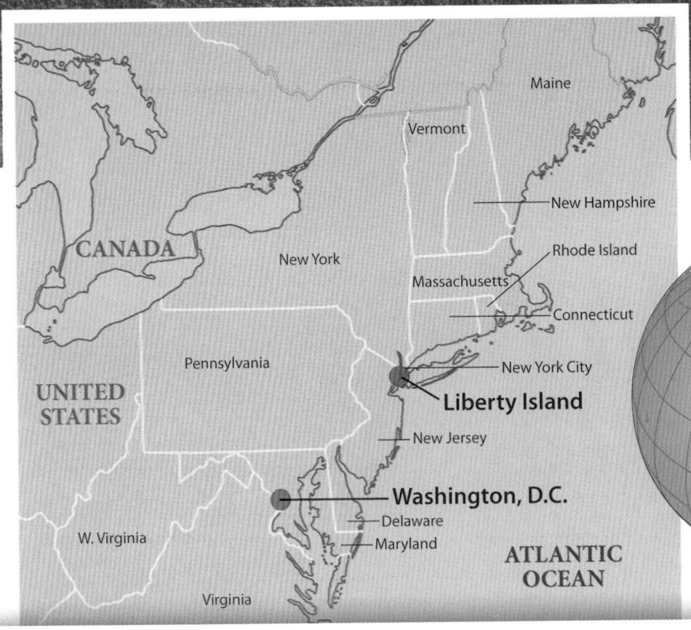
Maine
Vermont
New Hampshire
CANADA
New York
Rhode Island
Massachusetts
Connecticut
Pennsylvania
New York City
UNITED STATES
Liberty Island
New Jersey
Washington, D.C.
Delaware
W. Virginia
Maryland
ATLANTIC OCEAN
Virginia

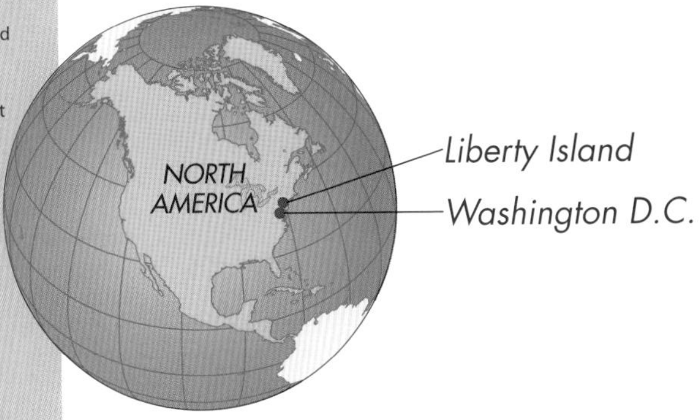
NORTH AMERICA
Liberty Island
Washington D.C.

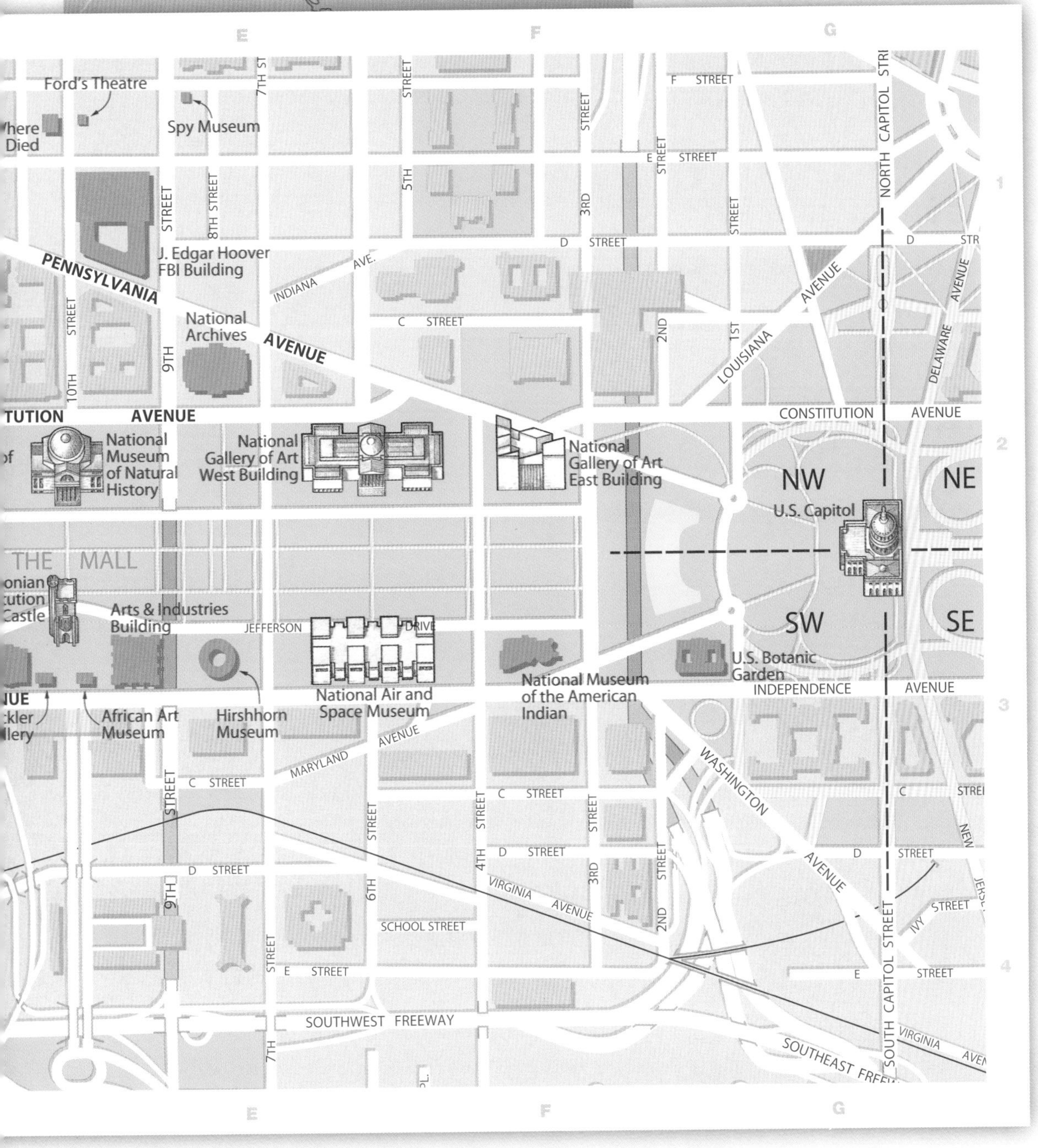
E
F
G
Ford's Theatre
Spy Museum
J. Edgar Hoover FBI Building
PENNSYLVANIA AVENUE
INDIANA AVE.
National Archives
CONSTITUTION AVENUE
National Museum of Natural History
National Gallery of Art West Building
National Gallery of Art East Building
LOUISIANA
DELAWARE AVENUE
NW
NE
U.S. Capitol
SW
SE
THE MALL
Arts & Industries Building
JEFFERSON DRIVE
National Air and Space Museum
National Museum of the American Indian
U.S. Botanic Garden
INDEPENDENCE AVENUE
African Art Museum
Hirshhorn Museum
MARYLAND AVENUE
WASHINGTON AVENUE
NORTH CAPITOL STREET
SOUTH CAPITOL STREET
VIRGINIA AVENUE
SCHOOL STREET
SOUTHWEST FREEWAY
1
2
3
4

Exploring Washington, D.C.

By Meg Runyan

For centuries, people have come to the United States seeking a new kind of government. Join kid explorer Meg Runyan as she explores the center of that government—Washington, D.C.

Invitation to Adventure

My friends were standing at the bus stop as Mom and I drove by. I couldn't help smiling. They were heading to school, and I wasn't.

I was about to spend three days exploring Washington, D.C. The adventure made history and social studies come to life. Here are some highlights from my trip.

The Heart of Town

Washington has many important places, but the Capitol is the center of town.

The first thing I noticed about the Capitol was its big white dome. I figured the dome was made of stone because so much of Washington is—wrong! The dome is actually made of nine million pounds of iron.

Beneath the dome is a large circular room called the Rotunda. Historic paintings and statues honoring famous Americans decorate this room.

There is an especially interesting statue of sixteenth President Abraham Lincoln there. As the story goes, President Lincoln hated posing for portraits. But because he had heard that the artist for the statue was poor, he decided to help her earn money.

U.S. Capitol

Lawmakers

All those statues and paintings are cool, but they're not why the Capitol matters. This famous building is home to Congress, the branch of our government that makes America's laws.

Congress has two parts: the Senate and the House of Representatives. The Senate has 100 members, two from each state. The House has over 400 members, with a different number from each state, depending on the size of the state's population.

Senators and representatives have challenging jobs because they help make the laws that everyone follows in the United States. A law starts off as a **bill**. If at least half of the members of Congress vote to approve it, the bill goes to the President.

If the President approves the bill, it becomes law. If he rejects, or **vetoes**, the bill, Congress can vote on it again. If two-thirds of each house approves it, then the bill becomes a law.

Washington Monument

Meg visits former Senator Jeffords.

The Gentleman From Vermont

While I was at the Capitol, I met former Senator Jim Jeffords from Vermont.

His goal has been "to make sure the U.S. does its best" for its people. Jeffords wants all kids to get a good education, and he believes deeply in protecting our environment.

Making laws isn't easy, I learned. Lawmakers have different ideas about what America needs, and getting lawmakers to agree takes lots of work and patience.

Former Senator Jeffords told me that when he got discouraged, he looked out his office window. Seeing the Capitol dome always **inspired** Jeffords and reminded him that we can get something done.

A Day with the Presidents

Not surprisingly, Washington is a great place to learn about our Presidents. Throughout the city, **monuments** help visitors remember important leaders.

We started at the Franklin Delano Roosevelt Memorial. After walking through the memorial, Mom and I decided to rent a paddleboat.

From the boat, we got a great view of the Jefferson Memorial. Standing in the center of the memorial is a statue of Thomas Jefferson, our third President and the primary author of the Declaration of Independence.

From the water, we also saw the Washington Monument. When finished in 1884, it was the tallest structure on Earth. Even today, the Washington Monument rises above the city.

That seems right to me. After all, no one else holds the same place in American history. George Washington was the first President of the United States, and he decided where the capital city should be built.

Jefferson Memorial

The White House at night

Lincoln Memorial

The President's House

Our next stop was the White House, which has been our President's home since 1800.

The White House has undergone many changes over the years. Perhaps the biggest change happened during the War of 1812, when America and England were fighting.

In August 1814, British forces invaded Washington, D.C., and President James Madison and his wife fled the city. British troops then burned the White House.

Afterwards, the White House had to be almost completely rebuilt, creating the oldest parts of the building we know today.

It's Over Already?!

I wish I had more time to explore the White House, and all the amazing parts of Washington, D.C. Still, my trip gave me a deeper understanding of how the United States works, and it made me feel **proud** to be a part of this great country.

Wordwise

bill: proposed law

inspire: to cause someone to have a positive feeling or emotion

monument: structure built so people remember a person or event

proud: showing self-respect

veto: reject a proposed law

Built to Inspire

Inspire yourself to answer these questions about U.S. monuments.

1. How did the United States get the Statue of Liberty? What do her torch and crown represent?
2. Name two ways that the Statue of Liberty has inspired people.
3. The President of the United States can veto laws. What does *veto* mean?
4. How is Meg Runyan changed by her visit to Washington, D.C.?
5. How are the Statue of Liberty and Washington, D.C., similar? How are they different?

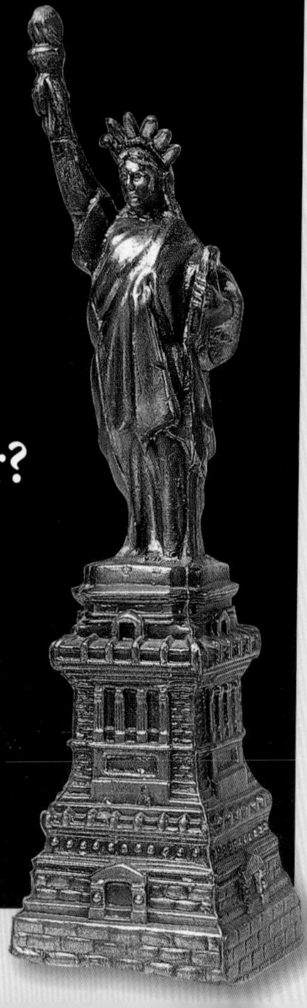